contemporary asian

BATHROOMS

Chami Jotisalikorn and Karina Zabihi
photos by Luca Invernizzi Tettoni

PERIPLUS

Published by Periplus Editions with
editorial offices at 130 Joo Seng Road
#06-01 Singapore 368357

ISBN-10: 0-7946-0479-X pb
ISBN-13: 978-0-7946-0479-0 pb

Distributed by:
North America, Latin America & Europe
Tuttle Publishing, 364 Innovation Drive,
North Clarendon, VT 05759-9436 U.S.A.
Tel: 1 (802) 773-8930; Fax: 1 (802) 773-6993
info@tuttlepublishing.com
www.tuttlepublishing.com

Asia Pacific
Berkeley Books Pte Ltd, 130 Joo Seng Road
#06-01, Singapore 368357
Tel: (65) 6280-1330; Fax: (65) 6280-6290
inquiries@periplus.com.sg
www.periplus.com

Japan
Tuttle Publishing, Yaekari Building, 3rd Floor
5-4-12 Osaki, Shinagawa-ku,
Tokyo 141 0032
Tel: (81) 3 5437-0171; Fax: (81) 3 5437-0755
tuttle-sales@gol.com

Printed in Singapore

10 09 08 07
6 5 4 3 2 1

the new asian bathroom: out of the closet

Not that long ago, the bathroom was but a utilitarian space, hidden from view within the inner recesses of the home. Part and parcel of western domestic architecture for several centuries, the general practice across Asia was to keep bathrooms a distance away from the living quarters. The concept of sitting in a tub, a common practice in the west and in the colder north Asian countries like Japan, was largely unknown and unnecessary in tropical Asia. The traditional Asian shower required only two items—a large urn and a scoop—and consisted of splashing bowls of rainwater over the body. Bathing took place outdoors where a breeze quickly dried the body after the bath.

The communal aspect of bathing in Asia is well rooted in ancient times, when the communal bath, like the Roman bath in Europe, was a place to congregate and socialize. Ancient Indian civilizations built capacious public bathing tanks that resembled enormous square or rectangular pools with steps leading down to wide landings where people performed their daily ablutions. These tanks were generally built into Hindu temple complexes, and were used in cleansing rites. These types of public bathing tanks were transported along with Hinduism to Bali, where similar baths can be seen today. In other parts of the Asian region, bathing and washing along the rivers and waterways were other forms of outdoor communal bathing.

The concept of an indoor bathroom that was part of the main house entered the tropical home only in the past century as Asians turned toward western living standards. Initially, scant attention was given to the design or comfort of the bathroom, since it was considered a functional space rather than an aesthetic one. Now, not only has contemporary Asian design embraced the concept of the bathroom as an art form, young designers in Asia are rapidly taking the lowly lavatory to a new level, with a creativity that continues to raise the bar.

Originating in Southeast Asia, tropical resort bathrooms came to the fore along with the tropical resort villa, thanks to the pioneering vision of Australian architect Peter Muller, whose design for the Oberoi Bali in the mid '70s represented a radical new concept in hotel design. Breaking away from the idea of a standard high-rise hotel room, he designed the hotel in the manner of a traditional Balinese village, with guests housed in traditional villas that offered bathrooms opening onto the outdoors as they would in a Balinese home. Considered sensational at the time, his concept has since then set the standard in tropical resort design. His designs for many of Bali's top luxury resorts, including the Amandari with its stunning pool, have influenced a stream of followers who have adopted the ethnic architecture approach and have taken it to new levels, as seen in the Four Seasons resorts and the Begawan Giri Estate in Bali. Over the decades, the concept of tropical resort villas, along with their exotic outdoor bathrooms has spread among resorts and spas, and to private homes around Asia and as far as the US.

Another key inspiration driving the new wave in bathroom design is the global spa movement that has gripped the new millennium. With the western world discarding their conventional pain-is-gain spa treatments for the holistic rejuvenation rituals long practiced in the east, the Asian-style spa has now become immensely popular.

Both homeowners and designers are currently strongly influenced by the luxury and beauty embodied in spa design, and its celebration of bathtubs, hot tubs, steam rooms, changing rooms, and all manner of state-of-the-art facilities for cleansing and cosseting the body.

right The warm tones of the counter top complement the vibrant color scheme in the bathroom. The frameless mirror and large windows and doors enhance the sense of a fluid, borderless space.

opposite The interplay of geometric shapes in this open air patio bathroom in Bali makes for a definitive modern statement. The ivory toned wall provides a dramatic backdrop for the green terrazzo of the vanity unit.

With buzzwords such as "wellness" and "pampering" echoing in our ears, the new approach to washing transforms the act of bathing from function to ritual. Likewise the humble bathroom has transcended from the utilitarian water closet to become something like a temple dedicated to body worship. Architects began to focus their attention on the bathroom's design, creating a space of beauty, style and atmosphere to relax the mind and delight the senses.

Some distinctively Asian-style spas have impressed upon people that a bathroom need not be the humdrum white-tile construction. Noteworthy examples include the Lanna Spa at the Four Seasons Chiangmai, designed to resemble a Thai temple, the Oriental Spa in Bangkok and the Aman Spa in Phuket, designed in the manner of classic Thai teak homes—these spas affirm the powerful use of interior design concepts and exotic materials in transforming the ordinary bathroom into luxurious fantasy worlds of style and sensuality.

With many of the world's most popular and exotic spas located in Southeast Asia, travelers and spa aficionados have been inspired to recreate the luxurious ambience of the Asian spa back in their homes. In Thailand, a new development that continues to fuel the spa bathroom craze is the trend for day spas located in renovated old houses; spa-goers who see the charming ways in which tubs and steam rooms have been installed in these old houses realize that similar renovations can be achieved in their own homes.

Two directions in contemporary Asian bathroom design are currently emerging: the tropical garden bathroom and the sophisticated urban bathroom. Bathrooms following the tropical garden direction have taken inspiration from the many resorts and spas in Bali and Thailand that offer idyllic outdoor bathroom suites. These emphasize the connection to nature, and rely on natural, earthy materials for visual impact and ambience. The beautiful garden bathrooms at the Begawan Giri Estate, designed by Singapore architect Cheong Yew Kuan, are a case in point. The villas are designed around a complex of pools and water features, each offering expansive outdoor bathroom suites with waterfalls, bamboo showerheads, tubs carved from boulders, and natural rock stepping stones, all set in the open air among a riotous profusion of ferns. Who wouldn't want to take a piece of such paradise back home with them?

In contrast to their tropical garden counterparts, urban-style bathrooms embody the western approach to bathroom design. They are enclosed within the dwelling, sometimes with no windows or direct access to the outdoors. The common element in urban bathrooms is a sense of high-tech glamor and minimalist chic, often making use of the latest in European design such as Arne Jacobsen fixtures combined with surfaces in stainless steel, glass, cement, resin, and marble. The pages of this book are adorned with impressive examples of this: a bathroom in a Bangkok penthouse has a tubular, stainless-steel shower stall with a grey stone-tiled floor and a glass door, a striking embodiment of uber sleek, masculine chic; in a Singapore residence, an all-white bathroom with a perfectly rectilinear tub seems too pristine for actual bathing, lest the addition of a human body mars the room's beautifully proportionate lines.

In both the urban bathroom and the tropical garden variety, designers have managed to retain a unique Asian identity, often by incorporating native materials into bathroom designs with innovation and imagination. In the Philippines, where coconuts are an abundant natural material, coconut shell tiles are used in bathroom ceilings and counter tops to

create an exotically textured surface that is rich in tone and soft to the touch. In Bali, gigantic stone boulders are scooped out and used as bathtubs, and wash basins are delicately lined with beautifully iridescent mother-of-pearl inlay. A bathroom floor in a Bangkok high-rise is lined with snow-white pebbles through which black stone tiles form a dramatic path to the toilet. In some bathrooms, everyday objects from the Asian household have been cleverly crafted into trendy bathroom fixtures. In a home in Bangkok, a wooden table is transformed into a bathroom counter with the addition of a sandstone wash basin and a copper faucet. At a beach resort in Thailand, a humble kitchen wok has taken on a new identity as a stylish wash basin.

Textures are important because they immediately add dimensions to the space. Plain white tiles have taken a step back while stone, terrazzo, glass, marble, wood, stainless steel and cement are now the hot new favorites among Asian bathroom designers. Glass-making techniques in Asia have developed to the point where vast panes and glass corners hitherto impossible now find their way into the contemporary Asian bathroom. Frosted green glass, once associated with retail design, adds sophistication and luxury while cement, an economical material, gives the edgy, industrial feel popular in minimal-chic bathrooms across Asia.

One of the more popular materials among designers in Asia is terrazzo. Used for centuries as flooring material, terrazzo is no newcomer to the design scene. The attractive, sleek, low-maintenance surface is versatile and economical, although extremely time-consuming to fashion. To manufacture terrazzo, marble or stone chips are embedded in concrete or cement that is cast and then smoothened and polished to a high sheen. Popular as an Art Deco flooring material in the

'20s, it became popular as a warm weather material and was used extensively throughout Florida and California in the '50s and '60s building boom. In Asia, terrazzo is the material of the moment, and has transcended from humble flooring to become increasingly fashionable as *the* material for custom-designed tubs, vanity counter tops, walls and seating; in some cases, entire bathrooms are outfitted in terrazzo.

Another popular trend in Asia is to feature different bathroom styles within one home, so that each bathroom has its own theme and color, mood and identity. After all, the most delightful aspect of designing bathrooms is their versatile, relatively small size and multitude.

There is definitely a move toward more creative and daring bathroom designs, fueled in part by the ease and habit of global travel. With access to diverse cultures and a new taste for international styles, both homeowners and designers find inspiration from all sources. Some Asian homes boast bathrooms fully kitted out with the last word in Italian design, such as Boffi limestone basins and tubs, Hansgrohe power showers, and Alessi ceramic fixtures, while others stick closely to local ethnic themes, installing items of traditional Asian décor such as antique hand-carved shutters and Japanese wooden tubs in homes nestled in bustling cities. Still other bathrooms exhibit a successful cross-fertilization of design lines, developing an "ethno-modern" approach. For example, an antique Indian door acquired from Kerala makes an alluring entrance to the creamy modern interior of a Kuala Lumpur bathroom that combines Indian antiques with Philippe Starck fixtures to delightful effect.

Undeterred by the restrictions of a metropolitan environment, designers and homeowners in Singapore and Bangkok have succeeded in merging part of the bathroom with the

right The round, green tinted glass wash basins against the marble counter top add a touch that is elegant yet playful and fun at the same time, cleverly enhanced by the halo of filtered light shining through the glass. **below** The shadow of the louvers adds interest to the simple and elegant combination of marble, glass and mirror in this bathroom. The cool white marble of the counter top is enhanced by the dark colored accessories, and the linearity of the design, by the rounded outlines of the sink, glasses and toiletries. **opposite** With its clean lines and geometric shapes, this bathroom has a definite masculine charm about it.

outdoors, whether through the use of outdoor showers, sliding doors, or picture windows that open out to lush gardens. In one Bangkok penthouse the bathtub is located on an open balcony, with a sliding glass wall partitioning off the bedroom on the other side, allowing the owners to enjoy an outdoor soak with a view of the city spreading below them. Heavily influenced by Southeast Asia's stunning tropical resorts and spas, city sybarites in metropolitan Asia are now insisting on outdoor showers in their metropolitan homes and high-rise apartments, with the trend traveling further afield to Florida, California and around the US.

Contemporary Asian bathrooms are riding the crest of a new wave of creativity and inspiration, as homeowners become more discerning about design and more demanding in their lifestyle habits. Asian décor motifs, with their serene lines, subdued grace and luxury of texture, have become intrinsic to the overall concept of the bathroom as sanctuary. Now a new status symbol of luxury living, the once secluded, boxed-in water closet has come a long way.

going for glamor A combination of luxurious elements creates the look and feel of Hollywood opulence in this cavernous master bathroom created by IA49 for the Bangkok home of businessman Raymond Eaton.

above Wide marble steps give
the generous bathtub the feel
of a personal spa. The mirrored
wall doubles the space for
those who like living large.
left Both floor and ceiling are
covered with white marble tiles
from Italy, creating a pristine
white surrounding—the perfect
backdrop for the artwork taking
center stage. On the wall hangs
a glazed ceramic sculpture by
a local artist, which the owner
purchased in 1993. He bought
the Philippe Starck stool much
later but its curved lines and
bold colors complement those
of the sculpture to serendipitous
perfection. The state-of-the-art,
high-tech scale is made by
Soehnle, and the glass basins
were imported from the US.

fantasy & fishes   Water is without doubt integral to any bathroom. This powder room created by Singapore-based designer Benny Cheng of space_craft offers the latest in innovative design and creative use of an outdoor–indoor space.

above This ethereal glass vanity unit is pure design genius. When the tap is turned on, the water forms a mirage hovering above the pond. Accessories from The Natural Source provide the finishing touch.

left The garden and pool area lie behind the "floating" mirror in the bathroom. The deck provides a perfect setting for unusual stone vases.

right The use of granite for the walls and floors creates a seamless transition from the bathroom to the outside pool area. The unique glass basin means guests can look down into the pond. "I like the way it surprises," says Benny Cheng. "What we did was to turn a little tunnel space into a feature of the home."

bathroom as temple
The owners of the grand Villa Ylang Ylang in Bali have taken hedonism to new heights with this luxurious master bathroom that is part modern Roman bath, part tropical sanctuary.

above The blue sculptured stone and wooden latticework vanity unit emulates the stone used in the sunken pool of the master bathroom. Tortoiseshell boxes are filled with hand towels and the large mirror framed in dark wood reflects and enhances the space. Customized accessories and bright flowers add the finishing touches.

right The little details we include in our bathrooms reflect our individuality and personality. Here a modern Balinese urn makes an unusual vase for these delicate, richly colored flowers.
opposite The attraction of this master bathroom can be found in its modern Roman spa feel. Palimanan stone inlaid into black pebbles sets the color palette of the space. Recessed lighting casts a soft glow over the sunken bath adorned with flowers. A large statue with its own landscaped pool behind the bath completes the picture.

assorted flavors The novelty of having multiple bathrooms in one house widens homeowners' design options. The four bathrooms in this Bangkok penthouse each reflects a different mood and theme, from country classic to futurist chic.

top This stall is a fantastic metal cylinder made of brushed steel that is all space-age cool.
above Wood and earthenware evoke the atmosphere of an old-style Japanese *ryokan*, or inn.
left Cement walls, stainless-steel fixtures and a glass counter, the standard bearers of masculine chic, fit perfectly with the city setting outdoors.
right Traditionally eastern in use, pebble and stone make unusual companions to modern Italian sanitary ware in this distinctly Japanese design.

above The shower and toilet are encased behind sleek glass panels, elevating them from items of mundane everyday life to elegant display objects.
left The bathtub fits snugly into an alcove. Placed on stone steps and adorned with gold lacquer accessories, Hermes bath towels and candles, the bath becomes a luxurious and glamorous retreat.
below Raw brick walls and recessed vertical apertures echo the elegant symmetry of Thai temple ruins. A counter top of dark wood continues the theme while adding a warm and earthy color to the room.
opposite A landscape mural cleverly compensates for the lack of a window in this powder room, transforming a square cube into a vast rice paddy. The theme here is of a Thai country bathroom, with weathered wooden planks suggesting a rural farmhouse floor and a classic rainwater urn of the type traditionally used in country baths remodeled into a wash basin for city dwellers.

the look is luxe Space is often at a premium in central Bangkok high-rises. The challenge of turning a cramped bathroom at Siri Sathorn Apartments into a haven of stylish luxury led interior designer Carolyn Corogin of C2 Studio to this approach.

left Echoing the atmosphere of a luxury boutique, the color and texture of frosted green glass make this small bathroom seem so inviting. The glass wall and door also let in natural light from the bedroom, brightening the windowless bathroom.
right To maximize the limited space, a glass wall separates the shower without obstructing the line of sight. The installation of tub, wall- and ceiling-showers gives the user a complete range of bathing options.
below The sink and fixtures are simple but elegant high-quality imports from Italy.

practical magic The bathroom is the one room in the house where practicality is a must. With the help of Sim Boon Yang of Eco-id Architects, these bathrooms are more than just user-friendly—they are a triumph of form and function.

above With its non-slip chiseled granite floor as well as oodles of ambient light, the shower is without doubt the highlight of the roomy master bathroom of this Singapore apartment. All-white accessories and soaps from The Natural Source offset the dark wood shelves and beige marble of the walls.

left This bathroom scale, found in a shop in Tokyo, is both funky and functional.

top right Bathed in soft lighting, the antique Burmese stoneware, which the owners rescued from a rubbish tip, is showcased in the separate toilet.

right This asymmetrical vanity table, paired with the mirror-fronted storage unit, creates an uncluttered transition between the master bedroom and bathroom, while giving uninterrupted views of the harbor beyond. Sliding doors maximize space.

opposite The master bathroom oozes quiet sophistication with its linear fixtures and fittings and soft beige granite. Made of planks of stained *chengai* wood joined together, the vanity unit resembles a butcher's block.

the color connection There's nothing elaborate in the design of this connecting bathroom. Design team IA49 plays with bold colors to liven up the small space, and the simple layout takes on a spontaneous character.

left The toilet and shower are separated by the partitioning wall in the middle of the room, which provides privacy from the two doors that give entry on both sides of the bathroom.

above The bathroom's bright color scheme complements the modern décor of the adjacent bedroom. A black marble counter top provides a dramatic contrast to the yellow tiled wall. The bulbous figure in papier mâché was bought on a whim at a local department store because its cheerful personality matched that of the bathroom.

tropical white   Cool shades of white present the perfect backdrop to the modern tropical look. The bathroom of this Balinese villa, with its unmistakable emphasis on simplicity, clearly belongs to the "less is more" school of thought.

above White and wicker create a tranquil and restful atmosphere in this space which is part en suite bathroom, part dressing room. The cleverly designed open shelves expose rows of wicker baskets to create the "minimalist storage" look. The unfinished brushstrokes of the paintwork on the mirror frame add an ethnic touch, while a bamboo ladder complements the overall look and provides a good holder for hanging towels.

right A large wicker basket is a great storage solution for rolls of white fluffy towels.
opposite Bali is blessed with the ideal climate for outdoor bathing. A white stone bath adds a touch of the modern and stone accessories enhance the lushness of the foliage beyond. A Balinese sculpture makes an unusual towel rail.

shophouse chic When is modern not too modern? These bathrooms retain the character of a Singapore shophouse while introducing sensual and luxurious elements to create a contemporary and understated opulence.

left Placing a bathtub under the window is an innovative use of a recessed niche. Tall flowers like these Birds of Paradise add height to the space and an exotic touch to any bathing experience. **below** The bathroom on the third floor of this shophouse has an unusual shape as it wraps the stairwell leading to the master bedroom. A Mappa Burle veneer around the vanity unit and the glow from concealed lighting render this a restful and luxurious room.

opposite The white glazed ceramic-tiled walls in this guest bathroom set off the decorative panels of mosaic marble and allow for detailing with wood. One of the main features of this bathroom is the frameless glass shower cubicle with the central green marble paneling. Playing on the green theme, the shelves showcase the medley of glass bottles. The floors are clad in Spanish textured sandstone.

masculine overtones The dark hue, symmetrical outlines and streamlined style of this guest bathroom give machismo appeal, while the splashes of color add a sense of irreverence—just the look IA49 envisioned for this bachelor pad in Bangkok.

left The sleek mirror, lamp, glass console and metal wash basin were brought from Italy by the owner, who shows an inclination toward urban sophistication. **opposite** What a difference a bit of color makes. A slim silhouette and matte black finish add an air of solemn power to the simple toilet. The owner's collection of Costa Boda Danish blown glass bottles and plastic Alessi legged bowls injects a touch of zest and humor to an otherwise serious "throne room."

sleek is sensual Clean lines and understated sophistication—tools employed by architects Antony Liu and Ferry Ridwan—transform the bathrooms at The Bale Hotel in Nusa Dua, Bali, into an oasis of cool, elegant calm.

above This bathroom literally steps down into the pool. "We wanted to make both pool and bathroom one unit to reduce the difference between the outside and inside," says Antony Liu. The stainless-steel towel rail adds sleekness to the space.
right The sculptural Axor taps are the ultimate in elegance and contemporary chic.
left The "floating" terrazzo vanity unit enhances the clean, modern feel of the bathroom. Simple ceramic accessories from Jenggala Keramik add the final touches.

surface story Cold forged metals are used extensively in the bathrooms at The Farm at San Benito—in this example, the round basin of polyurethane resin, and the ceiling lights made from ordinary water pipes are cold forged in bronze.

The dark colored walls made of terrazzo inlaid with mother-of-pearl give the bathroom the mysterious glamor of the starry midnight sky.

Tiles fashioned from pebbles are alternated with those made of natural granite to give the floor a textured contrast. The ceiling is fashioned from hand-cut coconut tiles.

seeing light Creating new dimensions in a square room is a challenge for any designer. This en suite bathroom by IA49 in Bangkok shows how cleverly positioned shelves, mirrors and doors and the use of translucent materials can do just that.

left A frosted glass panel is a clever way to divide the washing area and the bath and toilet area without sacrificing natural light. The cut-through shelf allows the space to flow unobstructed while adding visual interest. The dark wooden wall gives a sense of luxurious sophistication and the mirror reflects the window, doubling the natural light and further opening up the space.

top Sliding doors allow easy access from both sides between the bedroom and study. Frosted panels give a cool, contemporary edge while allowing more natural light into the bathroom from both sides.

above Opaque window tiles let in plenty of light while giving the user privacy in the bathroom, which is on the ground floor.

open-air option The top floor location of this Bangkok loft offers owners Vichien Chansevikul and Michael Palmer the luxury of an outdoor bathroom in the heart of the city, while an enclosed atrium provides privacy from neighboring buildings.

above Extremely high floor-to-ceiling glass walls let in sunlight and open up the narrow room. The toilet, located in a separate room, is accessible from both sides, and functions as part of the master bathroom and part of the guest powder room.

left Vichien designed the loft with all rooms connecting in a circular configuration around a central atrium. The left corner of the bathroom leads to a mirrored dressing room joined to the connecting corridor. Sliding glass doors allow access to the open air from all sides.

right A friend from Paris hand-carried these double ceramic wash basins in a suitcase to Bangkok. Hand-crafted leather toiletries containers by Leather Paragon lend a sophisticated, masculine look to the bathroom.

bathroom as art Inspired by the way African women in Ndebele paint their houses, artists Philip Lakeman and Graham Oldroyd used their bathroom as a blank canvas on which they created a wholly individual outdoor pamper room.

left Philip and Graham are constantly redesigning their Bali house. In its present incarnation, the open-air bathroom is an ode to art. The huge wall mural by the walkway, leading to an outdoor shower, is African in style.
below The vanity unit with the sunken sinks on a stainless-steel base was fashioned by the two artists. Graham's painting, entitled "My Laptop," is how "we communicate to each other these days," they say.
bottom Philip and Graham made everything, including these soap dishes and vanity box.

above This mirror with its elaborate ceramic frame was designed and made by Philip and Graham, and reflects the open-air shower area.
left "When we built the house, at first there was a bath," says Philip, "but we never used it, so it got ditched and we replaced it with an area to sit." Among their first acquisitions on arriving in Bali was this chair. "We loved it because it looked as if it was walking."

black magic   Black is back and looking cool. Nested in a converted shophouse along the east coast of Singapore, this industrial-style bathroom with a breakaway shower cubicle is a timeless classic—just what the owners and designers desired.

above Glass tiles that "break out" into the master bedroom, the sleek rain showerhead and the space-age shower nozzle complete the overall contemporary feel of this bathroom.

right Why enclose a powder room when a cleverly conceived panel of black mosaic tiles on an existing white wall works even better? This is a good example of economy and versatility. The stainless-steel accessories and sink are a continuation of the industrial theme found in the master bathroom.

left The chic combination of glass bricks, cement and black mosaic tiles lends an enduring spaciousness and ultimately sexy feel to the bathroom. The Chemistry design team artfully balanced the sleek look of the stainless-steel accessories with the soft mauve tones of the flowers and soaps from The Natural Source while, as Marcel Heijnen of Chemistry explains, "a subtle hint of blue-green is provided by the natural color of the glass used."

above The large sunken bath set in its own raised space in this treatment room is the definitive word in luxury. The teakwood louvered windows let in just the right amount of ambient light. Candles, an array of soothing lotions and potions and a color scheme that reflects the natural environment of Sentosa signal pure relaxation.

right The vanity bowls in the treatment room are constructed from a block comprising various types of granite, enhancing the color scheme. The wall-mounted taps, which have been imported from France, are contemporary and elegant.

spa modern

You are enveloped in a sense of well-being and luxury the minute you enter the Spa Botanica on Sentosa Island in Singapore. The earthy tones and soft lighting create a haven for those who believe in pampering their bodies.

Kathy Yuktasevi of the firm Leo Designers, who worked on the interiors of the Spa, wanted to "create an individual state-of-the-art shower and sculptural vanity area whilst maintaining a generic and organic feel of a relaxed sanctuary within the treatment rooms." The clever use of recessed lighting behind the mirror softens the ambience while the contrast of dark wood and natural tones of stone adds to the overall feel of indulgence. Green leaves enhance the sense of being close to nature.

out in the open   Enclosed villas give guests the luxury of an all-round outdoor
bathing and swimming experience at the Evason Resort & Spa Hua Hin in Thailand,
where bathrooms and pools are design features in the outdoor landscaping.

above While the sink and toilet areas are indoors, the outdoor shower and adjacent outdoor bathtub open straight into the lotus pond.

left The swimming pool terrace is found on the other side of the lotus pond and bathtub. The lush fringe of banana trees around the fence suggests a private hideaway.

opposite The lily pond, sunken bathtub and swimming pool merge seamlessly to form an integrated unit using innovative landscaping that combines style with function.

right Below the mirror, glass shelves provide ample storage room in the limited space. A bamboo ladder performs double duty as a towel rack.

below The gold hand-beaten metal basin adds an element of romance to the bathroom. Ordinary drinking water takes on an icy look in a pair of frosted glass bottles—enticing!

left At the Evason Resort & Spa Hua Hin, indoor bathrooms are a simple but elegant affair. Eva Shivdasani, who oversaw the design of the resort, fashioned the hanging cylinder lamps out of a material that resembles rawhide but is actually resin. Vertical windows flanking the mirrors open out to the outdoor shower on the other side.

symmetry for all seasons Using oodles of space and strong sculptural forms, architectural firm HYLA has designed a master bathroom perfect for the modern Singapore woman—cool, clean and ultimately covetable.

above Bright accessories from Lifestorey counterbalance the industrial look of the antique mirror and the concrete-and-Azul-limestone vanity unit. The aluminum light fitting is itself a sculpture, and the abundance of light enhances the outdoor feel.
left Little details such as these unusual soaps from Lifestorey add personality, élan and charm to any bathroom.

left and bottom right The rounded Hansgrohe tap and showerhead complement the linear contours employed in the master bathroom.
below The expansiveness of light and space is accentuated by floor-to-ceiling glass doors. A sliding window brings in more light from the air well.
below right The round shower cubicle contrasts with the rectilinear forms of the other fittings. The shower curtain, a pleasant departure from the usual glass enclosure, adds to the industrial yet elegant look.

tribal ablutions Inspired by a love of ethnic cultures gleaned from the owner's far-flung travels, this bathroom in landscape architect Bill Bensley's Bangkok home has a modern ethnic look which feels authentically earthy yet stylishly au courant.

above Natural stones in the wash basin echo the look of a babbling brook.

right An alcove for artefacts and an African tribal mask embody the concept of the bathroom as an art gallery.

opposite The unexpected and delicate elegance of the graceful ceramic wash basin, combined with the masculine chunkiness of the setting, is the subtle twist that injects a touch of modern sophistication to the otherwise primitive tableau.

the bare necessities   Creativity, daring and compatible materials form the basis
of good interior design. The design of the guest bathroom of this Kuala Lumpur
home questions "what constitutes the conventional expectation of 'being finished'."

left "I recall that when I was a child, all the bathrooms in the houses we lived in were simply finished in bare cement plaster, typical of the first generation of houses in Petaling Jaya from the 1950s and 1960s. If it worked then, why not now?" asserts homeowner and Malaysian architect Lillian Tay. The creative application of various shades of black gives the bathroom that sensual, "boudoir" quality. The polished Zimbabwe granite floor complements the clean cement walls and stainless-steel fixtures.

above The Nyatoh wood framed mirror softens and complements the counter top made from black Zimbabwe granite while the interplay of shapes and textures of the white lilies and brushed metal candle holder captivates the senses.

top right Details in contrasting colors make a stunning visual statement. An electric-blue Thai fighting fish in a tall glass vase completes the picture of effortless style.

above right The sleekness of the brush-finished stainless-steel bowl and cylindrical tap made from a chrome-plated brass pipe accentuates the richness of the enveloping black.

nirvana   Nature is central to the overall plan of this bathroom created by Eco-id Architects. The owners wanted "luxury in a garden setting," and what better way to bathe than in the company of birds flitting through the open space? Pure bliss.

above A 16th century figurine from Cambodia adds texture to white marble and porcelain.
left Fixtures and fittings, like this streamlined showerhead from Vola, enhance the quiet look of the bathroom. The symmetry of the identical bottles from Club 21 adds to the overall harmony.
opposite Veined white marble, a sunken Jacuzzi, an abundance of plants and the modern touch of a Corbusier lounger combine to create a light, airy space. "When we are in the shower during a rainy day," say the owners, "we feel that we are showering in the rain!" Three Indian urns and the stone sculpture reflect the owners' love of antiques.

on public display Outdoor restrooms seem to be the appropriate approach when the setting is the Evason Resort & Spa in Hua Hin, Thailand. The space is breezy and natural, complementing the beach resort location.

left In this lovely beachside restroom, the emphasis is on natural textures, such as raw wood, and unfinished touches, such as bumpy walls. Lines are both streamlined and simple.
below This quirky basin, made from an ordinary kitchen wok, is fashioned by creative director Eva Shivdasani, who decided it would make a unique and attractive wash basin.
opposite A raised roof over this open-air restroom allows sea breezes to pass through while offering protection from the elements. Mirrors mounted on pillars and glass counter tops enhance the atmosphere of a free-flowing space.

above "I have always loved designing bathrooms," confesses architect Shinta Siregar. Lombok-weave paneling on the storage units and traditional *banji* screens combine with modern fixtures to create a peaceful ambience.

right The white terrazzo sinks soften the dominant palette of dark timber and black terrazzo employed by interior designer Jaya Ibrahim.

opposite "Bathing is always an experience in the tropics," says Shinta. Made of terrazzo, the bathtub perched at the end of a wooden deck injects modernity into the private garden.

that quality time   Attention to detail and the seamless blending of traditional motifs with modern opulence lend these bathrooms at The Club at The Legian Hotel in Bali a classic elegance and serene ambience.

the luxury of space   Designed by IA49, this spacious master bathroom in the
Bangkok home of lawyer Andreas Richter and his wife, Petcharat, offers ample
breathing, brushing and bathing room for the busy couple who share it.

above Double sinks and a long
counter provide plenty of space.
The mirror reflects the garden
view and visually enlarges
the already ample dimensions.
left Floor-to-ceiling windows
are a rare luxury in most homes.
In this lucky couple's suburban
abode, these windows open the
room to the greenery outdoors,
creating an airy and wonderfully
relaxing atmosphere.
right A glass partitioned shower
stall keeps the interior space
unobstructed, maintaining the
luxuriously open feel.

living it up downtown   Effortlessly glamorous and seriously stylish, these
modern bathrooms at Bali's Downtown Apartments provide everything the
well-heeled traveler could possibly need for unwinding and indulging the senses.

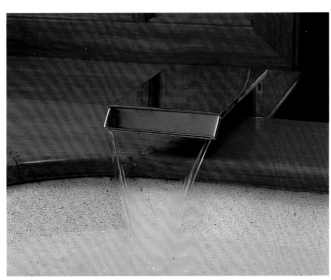

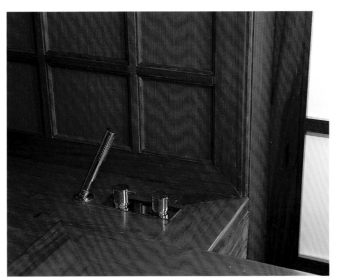

left This ultra-modern tap is an artwork in itself, and an example of the designer's meticulous attention to detail.
below left These taps are the ultimate in minimalist chic.
below Toilet rolls find their place in a storage unit of dark wood.
opposite Two bathrooms, one the mirror image of the other, are linked by a sunken terrazzo bathtub. The dark wood flooring, teak paneling on the walls and wooden base of the vanity unit are offset by a panel of mosaic to create a modern look.

reflections on nature The skilful use of bamboo, suspended mirrors and lighting transforms this master bathroom of a house in Singapore into a haven of harmony and tranquility, winning kudos for LATO Design.

The first thing that greets the eye upon entering the bathroom is the wall of bamboo. The designer wanted to give the bathroom an outdoor look with minimum enclosure. The bathroom and the adjacent bedroom take up the whole front facade of the house. The planter box provides essential privacy. The vanity counter and mirror are suspended, allowing users an unobstructed view of the bamboo. Discrete lighting under the bamboo creates a romantic mood at night, and the light reflects off the cool grey granite walls and floor. Accessories from The Link and Lifestorey add to the dreamy feel.

visual effects   Take a visual theme—such as an arc and a line—and add to it space and texture. Design team 1A49 did just that in this Bangkok home, creating a bathroom that amuses the eye and offers a cheerful place to get clean.

above Echoing the arc on the shower door, black-and-white checked tiles form a whimsical circle inside the shower stall. The blue glass wash basin was brought over from the US.

right The slant-and-circle theme is introduced on the door of the bathroom and is developed in its interior. Nearby sits a classic 1950s chair designed by Harry Bertoia for Knoll. The painting is the work of contemporary Thai artist Kongpat Sakdapitak, who is known for working in found objects and mixed media.

left The basic black-and-white color scheme brings a yin–yang balance to the contrasting slant-and-circle design theme. The frosted arc on the shower door complements the slanted edge of the marble partition.

pearls of the orient   Using a variety of different materials and the beauty of the immediate natural environment, the owner of this villa in Sanur, Bali, has created a bathroom that is at once both a secret garden and a stylishly modern sanctuary.

left The beautiful foliage that envelopes the antique door frame gives one the impression of being in a magical and secret garden. The marble walkway and seating area is offset by the lawn of black pebbles. The highlight of the bathroom, without doubt, has to be the mother-of-pearl basin set into the white coconut shell vanity unit.

above Mother-of-pearl and coconut shell is a wonderfully lavish combination of the delicate and sensual. Echoing the materials used in the vanity unit in the master bathroom, the shimmering opulence of layered mother-of-pearl boxes complements the counter of intricately worked white coconut shell.

outside in   Opening the bathroom to the outdoors can be tricky in metropolitan residences, where privacy and space often clash with the layout, but design team IAW has succeeded with the sensitive use of windows in Rika Dila's Bangkok home.

left Vertical windows flanking the mirror let in natural sunlight on both sides, while the view of the garden opens up the narrow interior space. Streamlined glass and ceramic accessories from Habitat are styled by designer Chananun Theeravanvilai of Chime Design.
right Tropical palms provide a lush natural curtain outside this big shower window, while injecting fresh green life into the room's cool marble interior.

water wonderland A highlight of tropical living is the open-air bathroom, where bathing becomes a tranquil communion with nature. The master bathroom of this private villa in Bali introduces a whole new dimension to the outdoor soak.

above The pairing of wood and stone emulates the harmony of the tropical garden outdoors. Fluffy white towels complement the black terrazzo vanity unit while a wall-to-wall mirror reflects the pool opposite. Big wicker baskets on wrought iron stands and stone accessories contribute to the spaciousness of the bathroom.

left The sunken pool is made out of volcanic rock taken from Kintamani. Slender wooden columns emphasize the vibrance of the surrounding foliage. Two statues from Singaraja enhance the tropical nature of the space.

beyond bronze Call it contemporary colonial or just pure tropical heaven, this treatment room at the Spa Botanica in Singapore, created by Kathy Yuktasevi of Leo Designers, offers a singularly rich, glamorous and luxuriously cosseting experience.

above All stress drains away after a bath. This tap of French design enhances the shape and form of the brass tub.

left This magnificent, to-die-for brass tub—accentuated here by candles and a single sculptural form—embodies the essence of modern style and classic design.

opposite Louvered doors of teak let in just the right amount of romantic light and complement the stand-alone brass bathtub. A granite vanity bowl and large mirrors with concealed lighting add to the soothing ambience.

swathes of turquoise   With muslin drapes gently wafting in the soft tropical breeze and an unusual color scheme, this master bathroom of a villa in Bali designed by Valentina Audrito nicely encapsulates the pleasures of outdoor bathing with a definitive chill-out zone.

above The beauty of this Jacuzzi bath lies in the soothing, cool stone and the billowing muslin drapes that provide both privacy from the garden beyond and an air of romance. A green glass bowl by glass sculptor Seiki Torige adds an ethereal touch.
left A wooden ladle injects a rustic charm into this otherwise modern Balinese bathroom.

opposite Turquoise and mustard yellow set the eye-catching color scheme for this airy and open bathroom. A sumptuous day bed is great for those important moments of self-indulgence, while large wicker baskets echo the tropical feel of the open-air space. Framed in dark wood, the mirror above the vanity unit reflects the bathtub opposite.

wise man's magic Gentle lighting, earthy tones and the remarkable combination of stone and coconut tiles are the hallmarks of this bathroom in the Begawan Giri Estate in Bali, a jungle resort designed by Singapore architect Cheong Yew Kwan.

left The surrounding forest is clearly an inspiration for the design of this master bathroom. The large tub made from a block of Javanese stone takes center stage. The rough-hewn exterior contrasts delightfully with the smooth interior and the ceiling of delicate coconut tiles.

top A copper basin on a white coconut vanity unit enhances the natural tones of the room. **above** Soft illumination and the simply designed furniture create a restful ambience.

elegance of design Exuding a sense of understated luxury normally found in a 6-star hotel, the design of this bathroom in a Singapore apartment created by Calvin Sim of Eco-id Architects is one of clean and restrained lines.

 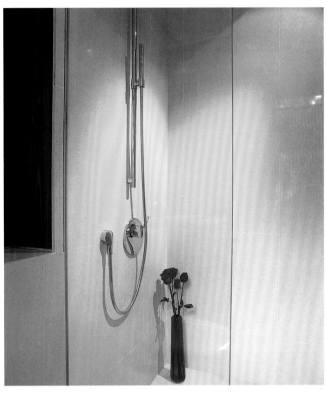

left "The overall feel is clean, using a limited palette of materials like French limestone and bleached reconstituted Canadian walnut veneer," says Calvin Sim. Large mirrors add depth to the space while soaps from The Natural Source and Philippe Starck taps complete the look.

above The naturally anodized aluminum screens above the French limestone bathtub let in optimum light and protect bathers' privacy. Accessories from The Natural Source and d'apres nous and white orchids enhance the luxury hotel atmosphere of this bathroom.

above The design of the guest shower room is sleek and simple and makes the most of the small space. Red accessories provide an added richness. The walls are fashioned from single pieces of Italian compressed marble in sandblasted finish.

the warmth of wood

Although it is unusual for a guest powder room to be so expansive, this one is big enough to double as the changing room for a nearby swimming pool. One door leads to an outdoor shower and a path leads to the pool.

left Subtle lighting and warm tones create a golden glow that flatters the complexion. The painting of a nude torso by Thai contemporary artist Acharn Aree matches the sculpture the owner bought on a trip to Vietnam.
right The owner had asked the designer to adapt the bathroom design from a magazine photo which he admired. The photo was not of a bathroom, which probably explains why the picture window and wood-paneled walls are a departure from the usual design elements seen in contemporary bathroom décor. The counter top and long bench offer generous "perch room" that comes in useful when guests are changing or grooming.

bed and bath Bathroom and bedroom become one at the Anantara Resort & Spa in Hua Hin, Thailand. Opening up the bath immediately adds a deeper dimension of luxurious space and light to the otherwise conventional hotel room.

above With the glass panels open, bathers can soak while enjoying the view of the garden beyond the balcony. The glass paneling separates the tub from the adjacent shower stall.

left Opaque sliding glass panels can be closed for privacy while still letting natural light into the bathroom. The use of terrazzo for the tub allows it to blend seamlessly with the bedroom wall without looking like a tub.

bali stage craft Clean, modern lines and an interesting exploitation of the indoor and outdoor space work beautifully with stage-like lighting, lending these bathrooms in a Balinese villa a cool ambience and impressive theatricality.

above A free-standing base topped with terrazzo and an ivory stone basin present an interesting introduction to the open-air shower room.
right The separate vanity area beyond the sunken bath not only heightens an impression of privacy, but also accentuates the splendor of the large Jacuzzi.
left The wooden shingles used in the roof are from Borneo and balance the stonework nicely. The teak Jacuzzi overlooking the Japanese-inspired garden adds a pleasing contrast to the open window. A bamboo ladder, also used as a towel rail, firmly places this bathroom in Bali.

the quality of space The owner of this condominium in Singapore was looking for a fuss-free, chic look when she completely redesigned the bathrooms in her home. The contemporary style is balanced with unusual sculptures and paintings.

above The use of glass and steel against dramatic black mosaic tiles lends this shower room a modern and yet masculine feel at the same time. The plethora of plants outside the bathroom window lets in subtle lighting which highlights the stillness of the space.

right The uniformity of the black mosaic and stainless-steel divide is simple yet pleasing to the eye. Using a time-proven trick, these large mirrors create the illusion of spaciousness.

left The use of white for the walls and vanity unit greatly enhances the size of this powder room and contrasts nicely with the dark wood above the loo. The round stainless-steel sink imbues a modern touch while the wooden soap dish, the Chinese paintings and beautiful sculpture from South Africa lend the space a signature style.

below The neutral tones of white and cream marble, light colored wood and Balinese accessories create a soothing atmosphere in this guest bathroom. Givenchy towels and soft lighting enhance the mood.

mosaic medley Colored tiles can be used to dramatic effect, adding life to even the simplest spaces. Designed by Bangkok's IA49, this bathroom may be colored in basic brown and beige, but the clever tiling creates energy and life.

above The simplicity of a basic round wash basin as well as minimalist fixtures complement the energetic tile pattern.

left Soaps with unusual textures and colors can come in handy as décor elements, enhancing the color scheme of any bathroom. These funky herbal soaps are from Harn Products.

opposite A recessed shelf keeps surface lines clean in this narrow room and a partial wall hides the shower. A glass panel acts as a shower curtain, letting in light and extending the space.

simply modern Simplicity is always seductive. Clean lines and an innovative use of textures and fittings lend a serenity and sophistication to these bathrooms in a Singapore house designed by K2LD Architects.

above The infinite possibilities of limestone are fully explored in the walls, vanity unit and tub. The wall-to-wall mirror above the sink accentuates the spaciousness of this master bathroom.
right This powder room may be small but the custom-made limestone sink and unusual tap give it plenty of character.
far right Cleverly concealed lighting behind the mirror sets off the one-of-a-kind tap made from a stainless-steel pipe.
opposite The limestone tub and shower with cut-out ventilation holes bestow on the bathroom a strikingly monastic modernity.

al fresco bathing
Thailand's tropical heat provides the perfect incentive for the outdoor soak. This bathroom suite at the Anantara Resort & Spa Hua Hin by Bangkok-based Bensley Design Studios evokes luxury using color and texture.

above This outdoor wash stand is made of orange terrazzo. The rock basin is lined with pebbles, reminiscent of a brook bed. The green patina on the mirror and faucet has an antiquated look, contrasting with the thoroughly contemporary shapes.
right Slabs of black stone form a textured background for a sculptural wall lamp that could pass for an art installation.
left Sensuous frangipani blossoms never fail to add a beckoning appeal to the bath. Warm orange terrazzo lends a soft and inviting atmosphere to the outdoor tub surrounded by a floor of black stones. Water trickles from two spouts designed to resemble old-fashioned pumps.

above Water cascades into the tub from a rough-hewn stone tap, mimicking a country well. Tap handles are located on a wide terrazzo edge, which also serves as counter space for bathers. The recessed panel frames a wall light.

left These high walls give the outdoor shower a feeling of guarded seclusion.

opposite The steam room is housed in a separate walled enclosure with an outdoor shower. Inspired by the design elements found in classical Thai architecture, the tall wooden double doors mimic those of a Thai temple while the mottled green patina on showerheads and handles lends an air of antiquity, though the shapes and lines are contemporary.

draped in luxury Inspired by the open-concept bathrooms at resort hotels, Sim Boon Yang of Eco-id Architects and the owners of this house in Singapore have achieved the airiness of an open-plan space.

top The coolness of the marble table top is accentuated by the Philippe Starck vanity bowl, the linearity of the Vola tap, and the celadon accessories and soaps from Anthropology Homeware.

above "We've always liked white bathrooms because they give a sense of space, light and purity," say the owners. White walls, tub and streamlined fixtures give the room plenty of style.

left The double layers of silver and gold in these curtains add rich warmth and texture to the well-designed space.

stone works Perched on a hill in Uluwatu, Bali, this house, designed by Guiseppe
Verdacchi is built on the site of an old limestone quarry. The bathrooms make creative
use of the surrounding stone, and are a testament to the concept of preservation.

left This unusually shaped tub, positioned majestically on the balcony, offers incredible views of the surrounding countryside.
below Unexpected shapes, brightly colored accessories, and the combination of varying textures add to the overall bold and dramatic atmosphere of this open-air bathroom.
below left The soft tones of the ivory stone produce an interesting textural contrast to the basin centered on rough-hewn limestone columns standing where they were found in the quarry.
opposite The wall, hand-crafted in limestone, doubles as an impressive sculptural form and waterfall in this bathroom. The sunken bath sits in a "moat" surrounded by wooden columns and tropical foliage. A music stand makes an unusual toilet-roll holder.

107

gallery space Minimal design can create maximum impact, as seen in this simple but stunning powder room created by IAW for a Bangkok home. When forms are simple, the trick is to play with textured surfaces.

left The white-on-white color scheme is balanced by the contrasting textures of the smooth wash basin and the tiled wall, while a bold raspberry-red wall suggests high drama. Styled by Chananun Theeravanvilai of Chime Design, waffle-weave towels echo the pattern of the tiled wall, while round candle holders from Habitat balance the severity of straight lines.
right A mirrored wall adds the illusion of depth, reflecting the picture window. The bathroom also functions as a mini gallery displaying the owner's collection of ceramic vases, modern Thai paintings as well as an antique Tibetan rug.

a touch of kerala   Create a whole new facet of modernity with a few carefully chosen pieces, such as these Indian antiques, which add an exotic touch to the contemporary bathrooms of this Kuala Lumpur house designed by Ernesto Bedmar.

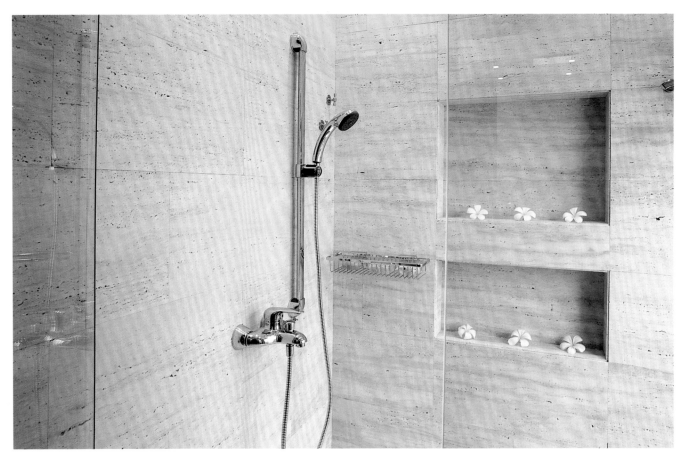

above A Hansa showerhead and hewn shelf units give the roomy shower cubicle a minimalist feel. **left** An antique Indian wooden cow head—for good luck—and a silver bracelet for the guest towel add a quixotic touch. **right** This powder room gracefully combines innovation and tradition. A rough-hewn slab of unpolished granite sits on a *balau* wood vanity counter. The antique doors of solid jackwood, traditionally installed at the main entrance of a Kerala house, are a perfect counterpoint to the cool, modern interior. The walls are clad in unfilled travertine marble while the floors are laid with in-filled travertine marble.

a sensuousness of space   "Having the whole bathroom white greatly enhances the space and luminance of the room. Corners appear seamless and the space is visually enlarged," says designer Benny Cheng of space_craft.

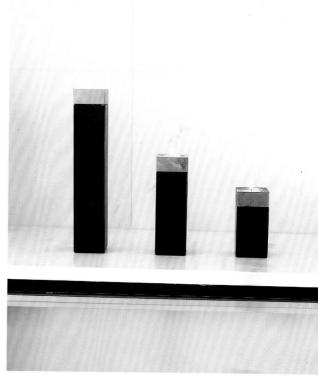

above Keep accessories simple to maximize the contours of a room. These dark wooden night-light holders add texture and elegance to the Volakas marble walls and glass-fronted walnut storage cabinet, enhancing the overall sensuality of the space.

left The creamy white Italian marble lends a luxurious feel to the bathroom. The Hansgrohe taps designed by Philippe Starck add to the contemporary look of the bathroom while white accessories complement the sense of tranquility provided by the greenery. Nothing can beat a rain shower in the large walk-in cubicle for the ultimate in pampering.

clean lines are for living The juxtaposition of dark and light in this master bathroom creates an ultimately masculine yet soothing feel. Accessories are carefully chosen to accentuate the impression of an inviting, user-friendly bathroom for two.

left One of the signature styles of K2LD Architects is the clever use of concealed illumination. In this case, lighting was employed behind the mirrors and under the black granite vanity unit. Here, the architects wanted "maximized lighting coming through."

above Playing with lines and shapes is always an interesting approach to designing a bathroom. The Toto taps above the flat, round Scarabeo basins from Italy accentuate and mirror the contours of this shaving set, a must-have for any gentleman.

sun salutation Designed by IAW, the master bathroom of businesswoman Rika Dila's Bangkok residence is completely configured to embrace natural light. The glass walls face eastward, drenching the room in the sun's rays every morning.

above The bathroom, with its long corridor and shower cubicle forming an "L" at the end, is built around an atrium conceived as an outdoor yoga and massage deck. Glass walls open out into the atrium, giving both light and privacy. A collection of Tibetan rugs injects color into the pristine white surroundings. **left** Bathing becomes a luxurious indulgence when it is done on a white marble pedestal. The bath, styled by designer Chananun Theeravanvilai of Chime Design, is decorated with candles from Habitat. A glass panel opens up the niche while letting light in from the adjacent toilet.

right Should fresh-air ablutions be needed, the shower has a glass door that leads to the atrium. A moat gutter drains water off the floor. Recessed shelves display a collection of sensuously curved buffalo horn cups from Habitat.

as time goes by   True modernity is timeless. Pairing simple lines with smooth stone, wood and a single piece of art, designer Chan Soo Khian of SCDA turns the master bathroom of a detached house in Singapore into a haven of tranquility.

left The wall behind the hydro-bath functions as a unique and dramatic alcove in which the owner has hung a wooden carving taken from a traditional house in Chiangmai. The piece of art was a gift from a friend. A triptych of vases with bright yellow flowers completes the spa-like feel of this area.
opposite "I love everything about the bathroom," muses the owner. "It is a total effect of serenity and calm. It is a place where I can relax and be unhurried." The beige honed granite wall and floor lend a tranquility and repose to the whole room. The ceiling of the bathroom is made from *chengai* wood strips which contrast pleasingly with the polished granite of the vanity top. The white accessories from The Natural Source add crispness to the overall design.

boffi beautiful   Sleek, sensual, and discerningly elegant, a Boffi bathroom says it all. These bathrooms showcased at Cream 136 in Singapore offers the last word in desirable designer bathrooms.

top This singular showerhead epitomizes a sleek and simple yet stunning design.
above The neat outlines and sheer sexiness of the shower-heads and taps accentuate the silky lines of the Corian bathtub.
left Black and white makes for an arresting combination. The stylishness of the Corian tub against Bisazza mosaic walls, analogous fixtures and the symmetry of sleek horizontal and vertical lines characterize this ultra-modern bathroom design.

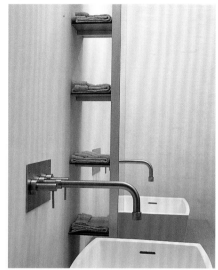

above Linearity is a signature of Boffi's designs. These square sinks in the Gobi series by M Wanders sitting on an oak vanity unit are definitive Boffi.

top right Neat shelves behind the mirror make a modish storage place for these Italian cotton towels.

above right Cream designer Tristan Tan has an unusual description for Boffi's creations: "yummy!" In this bathroom, he rendered the grey walls with cement to provide just the right backdrop for the all-white Boffi fixtures and accessories.

left The blueprint for the bathroom is sexy and masculine. A tall, slim mirror heightens the space while framing the Gel sink by Piero Lissoni and the towel rail from the Minimal series by G Gianturco.

above The purity of this ekotek-and-aluminum vanity unit by J Bernett for Boffi is an ideal solution for small spaces. The simple yet original box mirror and unique tap complement the linearity of the design.

above A vanity stand in dark, solid ash comes with trim storage drawers for stacking Italian cotton towels.
right The funky lamp adds an industrial touch. The sink is made of solid Bihara stone on an ash stand dyed a dark tone. A white ceramic soap dish by ER Palomba and a square cotton towel are the obvious choice of accessories.

it's all in the details Designing a modern living space has everything to do with highlighting an architectural style with complementary interiors and experimenting with the subtleties of textures, shapes and colors.

left This custom-made dark wood mirror and vanity unit offers a great place for adding design elements. Flowers that complement the wood and napkin rings used as towel holders create an unusual touch to the finish of this guest bathroom.

above The interior designer (kz designs) chose accessories in a dark color to offset the lighter shade of the tiles. The beige tiles on the floor and on one wall are made in Thailand and provide a contrast to the white ceramic tiles on the remaining walls. Moroccan tagine pots make unusual soap dishes.

tub of tranquility   At The Farm at San Benito in the Philippines, a lovely outdoor garden is transformed into an idyllic bathroom suite with the addition of a romantic tub made of cement and covered with bronze, using the technique of cold forging.

This garden could be anywhere, but an atmosphere of Eastern tranquility comes across with the combination of geometric shapes—the circle, triangle and rectangle are balanced with the dark and light colors of the tub and faucet. The simple bamboo wall not only protects bathers' privacy, it brings out the zen-like serenity found in the garden surroundings. The bathtub is fashioned using the method of cold forging, which requires no heat but allows any type of surface—ranging from cement to cardboard—to be forged with metal. This gives the designer much more artistic freedom to create innovative designs that would otherwise be impossible in metal, due to the prohibitive production costs or limitations of the material. The process uses real metals; bronze will acquire a patina and iron will rust, but both can be polished to their original state.

The authors would like to express their thanks to the following people who gave their kind support during the production of this book:

BALI
Glenn Parker, GKA Architects, Valentina Audrito, Cheong Yew Kwan, Gill Wilson, José Luis Calle at The Balé, Anjarini Kencahyati, Richard North Lewis of Stoneworks, Giuseppe Verdacchi, Joost van Grieken, Shinta Siregar of Nexus Studio Architects, Fredo Taffin of Espace Concept, Graham Oldroyd and Philip Lakeman of Pesamuan, Arthur Chondros and Daniel Collins at Downtown Apartments, Hansjörg Meier and Tomoka Yamamoto at The Legian, Antony Liu Budiwihardja, and Jaya Ibrahim.

Valentina Audrito email: vale-studio65@dps.centrin.net.id

Antony Liu Budiwihardja email: dwitunggalmandiri@yahoo.com

Espace Concept www.espaceconcept.net

GKA Architects Jl Raya Legian 362, Legian, Kecamatan Kuta 80361 Bali, tel: (62) 361 763 064

Guiseppe Verdacchi email: verdachi@indosat.net.id

Jaya Ibrahim email: jayaoffice@cbn.net.id

Jenggala Keramik www.jenggala-bali.com

Joost van Grieken email: Joost@idola.net.id

Nexus Studio Architects Perkantoran Duta Wijaya, Unit 1, Jl Raya Puputan, Denpasar Bali, tel: (62) 361 744 3493, email: nexus@edps.centrin.net.id

Pesamuan Jln Pungutan 25, Sanur Bali, www.pesamuan-bali.com

MALAYSIA
Gregory Dall of Pentago and Lillian Tay of Veritas Architects.

Pentago 21-11 The Boulevard, Mid-Valley City, Lingkaran Syed Putra, 59200 Kuala Lumpur, tel: (03) 2282 3188, email: pentago@po.jaring.my

Veritas Architects 148 Jln Ampang, Kuala Lumpur 50450, tel: (03) 2162 2300, www.veritas.com.my

PHILIPPINES
Mr Eckard Rempe of The Farm at San Benito.

SINGAPORE
Ernesto Bedmar of Bedmar & Shi, Calvin Sim and Sim Boon Yang of Eco-id Architects, Marcel Heijnen of Chemistry Design Pte Ltd, Lim Cheng Kooi and Tan Kok Hiang of Forum Architects, Guz Wilkinson of Guz Wilkinson Architects, Romain Destremau and Ko Shiou Hee of K2LD Architects, Lim Ai Tiong of LATO Design, Hund & Pups Design Studio, Hilary Loh and Han Loke Kwang of HYLA Architects, Kathy Yuktasevi of Leo Designers Pte Ltd, Benny Cheng of space_ craft, Chan Soo Khian of SCDA Architects, and Dr Stanley SH Quek of Region Development Pte Ltd.

Anthropology Homeware 16A Lor Mambong, Holland Village, S'pore 277677, tel: (65) 6467 2663, www.anthropology.com.sg

Bedmar & Shi 12A Keong Saik Rd, S'pore 089119, tel: (65) 6227 7117, email: bedmar.shi@pacific.net.sg

Chemistry Design 4 Everitt Rd, S'pore 428563, tel: (65) 6481 8589, www.chemistryteam.com

Club 21 Gallery Four Seasons Hotel, #01-07/8, 190 Orchard Blvd, S'pore 248646, tel: (65) 6887 5451, www.clubtwentyone.com

Cream #01-01–03, 5 Purvis St, S'pore 188584, tel: (65) 6333 9115, email: creamhome@pacific.net.sg

Cream 136 136 Bukit Timah Rd, S'pore 229838, tel: (65) 6836 3591, email: cream136@pacific.net.sg

d'apres nous 22 Duxton Hill, S'pore 089605, tel: (65) 6423 0655, www.d-apres-nous.com

Eco-id Architects 11 Stamford Rd #04-06, Capitol Bldg, S'pore 178884, tel: (65) 6337 5119, email: ecoid@pacific.net.sg

Fluv Floral Stylists 66 Club St, S'pore 069440, tel: 6536 8806, www.fluv.com.sg

Forum Architect 47 Ann Siang Rd #06-01, S'pore 069720, tel: (65) 62 24 2778, www.forumarchitects.com

Guz Wilkinson Architects 14B Murray Terrace, S'pore 079525, tel: (65) 6224 2182, www.guzarchitects.com

Hund & Pups Design Studio 10 Defu Lane 1, S'pore 539485, tel: (65) 6281 1586, email: hundnpups@ yahoo.com.sg

HYLA Architects 47 Ann Siang Rd, #02-01, S'pore 069720, tel: (65) 6324 2488, www.hyla.com.sg

K2LD Architects 136 Bukit Timah Rd, S'pore 229838, tel: (65) 6738 7277, www.K2LD.com

kz designs tel/fax:(65) 6836 3365 www.kzdesigns.com

LATO Design 520 Balestier Rd #04-00, Unit 7 Leong On Bldg, S'pore 329853, tel: (65) 6475 7571, email: latodesign@yahoo.com.sg

Leo Designers 219 Henderson Rd #09-03, S'pore 159556, tel: (65) 6272 7371, fax: (65) 6276 3977, email: leo@lidgintl.com

Lifestorey Pacific Plaza #04-01, 9 Scotts Rd, S'pore 228210, tel: (65) 6737 7998, www.lifestorey.com

SCDA Architects 10 Teck Lim Rd, S'pore 088386, tel: (65) 6324 5458, www.scdaarchitects.com

space_craft 2b Mount Emily Rd, S'pore 228484, tel: (65) 6333 3108, www.spacecraft.com.sg

The Link Boutique #01-10 Palais Renaissance, 390 Orchard Rd, S'pore 238871, tel: (65) 6737 7503, www.TheLink.com.sg

The Natural Source B1-52 Wisma Atria, 435 Orchard Rd, S'pore 238877, tel: (65) 6235 0420, www.thenaturalsource.com

The Touch 38 Bukit Pasoh Rd, S'pore 089852, tel: (65) 6325 4990, www.thetouch.com.sg

X.TRA Living 9 Penang Rd, #01-01 Park Mall, S'pore 238459, tel: (65) 6336 0688, www.xtra.com.sg

THAILAND
Rika Dila, Chananun Theeravanvilai of Chime Design, Raymond Eaton, Mr and Mrs Andreas and Petcharat Richter, Diana Moxon of Anantara Resorts, Vichien Chansevikul and Michael Palmer, Brian Renaud, Carolyn Corogin of C2 Studio, Bill Bensley of Bensley Design Studios, Eva Malmstrom Shivdasani of Six Senses Resorts & Spas, H Ernest Lee, Lyndon Discombe and Jintana Prachuabmoh of Evason Resort & Spa Hua Hin, Worapan Opapan of Origins, Marie-Eve Cadouin of Ytsara, Tony Supattranont of Harn Products, Khun Jeerapa of Anyroom at Siam Discovery Center Bangkok, Khun Jeab of Habitat Bangkok, and Cocoon Bangkok.

Anyroom 4th Floor Siam Discovery Center, Bangkok 10330, tel: (662) 658 0583, fax: (662) 658 0584, www.anyroom.com

Bensley Design Studios 57 Sukhumvit 61, Bangkok 10110, tel: (662) 381 6305, www.bensley.com

C2 Studio The Prime Building, Level 15, Suites B&C, 24 Sukhumvit 21, Bangkok 10110, tel: (662) 260 4243, fax: (662) 260 4316, email: Carolyn@c2studio.net

Chime Design 5th Floor, 2/4 Wireless Rd, Bangkok 10330, tel: (662) 6554 2445, email: chananun@chimedesign.com

IA49 81 Sukhumvit 26, Bangkok 10110, tel: (662) 259 3533/260 4370, email: ia49@49group.com, www.49group.com

IAW 27/1 Sukhumvit Soi 53, Bangkok 10110, tel: (662) 713 1237, email: iawbkk@loxinfo.co.th

Habitat Bangkok 4th Floor Siam Discovery Center, 989 Rama I Rd, Patumwan Bangkok 10330, www.habitat.net

Harn Products 4 Patanaves 2, Sukhumvit 71, Bangkok 10110, tel: (662) 711 1812, fax: (662) 711 2604, email: marketing@thann.info, www.harnproducts.com

Origins The Emporium, Sukhumvit 24, Klongtoey Bangkok, tel: (662) 664 8282

Ytsara 147/6 Soi Samahan, Sukhumvit Soi 4, Bangkok 10110, tel: (662) 656 7060, email: info@ytsara.com, www.ytsara.com